THE MORNING BITE

A BASS FISHING DEVOTIONAL

Blake Smith
with **James Niggemeyer**
and **Chris Wells**

Copyright © 2023 Blake Smith with James Niggemeyer and Chris Wells.

All rights reserved. No part of this book may be used or reproduced by any means, graphic, electronic, or mechanical, including photocopying, recording, taping or by any information storage retrieval system without the written permission of the author except in the case of brief quotations embodied in critical articles and reviews.

WestBow Press books may be ordered through booksellers or by contacting:

WestBow Press
A Division of Thomas Nelson & Zondervan
1663 Liberty Drive
Bloomington, IN 47403
www.westbowpress.com
844-714-3454

Because of the dynamic nature of the Internet, any web addresses or links contained in this book may have changed since publication and may no longer be valid. The views expressed in this work are solely those of the author and do not necessarily reflect the views of the publisher, and the publisher hereby disclaims any responsibility for them.

Any people depicted in stock imagery provided by Getty Images are models, and such images are being used for illustrative purposes only.
Certain stock imagery © Getty Images.

ISBN: 978-1-6642-8967-3 (sc)
ISBN: 978-1-6642-8966-6 (e)

Library of Congress Control Number: 2023901025

Print information available on the last page.

WestBow Press rev. date: 2/7/2023

Scripture quotations marked KJV are from the Holy Bible, King James Version (Authorized Version). First published in 1611. Quoted from the KJV Classic Reference Bible, Copyright © 1983 by The Zondervan Corporation.

Scripture quotations marked ESV are from the ESV Bible® (The Holy Bible, English Standard Version®), copyright © 2001 by Crossway Bibles, a publishing ministry of Good News Publishers. Used by permission. All rights reserved.

Scripture quotations marked NIV are taken from the Holy Bible, New International Version®, NIV®. Copyright © 1973, 1978, 1984 by Biblica, Inc.™ Used by permission of Zondervan. All rights reserved worldwide.

Scripture quotations marked NLT are taken from the Holy Bible, New Living Translation, copyright © 1996, 2004, 2007 by Tyndale House Foundation. Used by permission of Tyndale House Publishers, Inc., Carol Stream, Illinois 60188. All rights reserved.

Scripture quotations marked CSB have been taken from the Christian Standard Bible®, Copyright © 2017 by Holman Bible Publishers. Used by permission. Christian Standard Bible® and CSB® are federally registered trademarks of Holman Bible Publishers.

Scripture quotations marked HCSB®, are taken from the Holman Christian Standard Bible®, Copyright © 1999, 2000, 2002, 2003, 2009 by Holman Bible Publishers. Used by permission. HCSB® is a federally registered trademark of Holman Bible Publishers

PREFACE

In tournament fishing, one of the most propelling things that can happen on tournament day is getting that "morning bite." It calms your nerves and gives you peace in knowing that no matter how the rest of the day goes, you already have everything you need for success that day.

When the three of us got together to write this book, we agreed on a few things about what we wanted to do. First, we wanted to bring together our love of two things, faith and fishing.

Second, we wanted people to be able to obtain their "morning bite" spiritually through a light read that would tie scriptures in with stories from our lives in the world of professional fishing.

And finally, it was our goal to help readers expand beyond the scriptures in this book to find their own way of developing a love for the Word of God and how it applies to everyday life.

We hope you enjoy it!

Blake Smith

2 CORINTHIANS 4:16–18

(N I V)

> Therefore we do not lose heart. Though outwardly we are wasting away, yet inwardly we are being renewed day by day. For our light and momentary troubles are achieving for us an eternal glory that far outweighs them all. So we fix our eyes not on what is seen, but what is unseen, since what is seen is temporary, but what is unseen is eternal.

In fishing, it is easy to find ourselves continually shifting our focus to ensure we don't miss a key detail. There could be a big bass on a bed, or a blue heron a hundred yards down the bank that keeps feasting on a shad spawn that you didn't know about. Fishermen have an ability to be hyper focused at any given moment. This intensive focus can be a very useful tool when fishing tournaments but wreak havoc on our spiritual lives.

I spent many years of my life focused on the pursuit of catching fish and completely missed the mark on my calling. God orchestrated my fishing career not just to catch fish but to catch people for His glory. One of the biggest lessons I have learned over the past few years is to focus on God, His Word, and how I can best serve Him, and everything else will fall into place.

If we take our focus off Jesus, we are prone to wander and be distracted. We will miss the best gift in this life, which is a relationship with Jesus Christ. Today, try making Him your focus, and hold on. Sometimes we think we're on course, but we can't see past the distractions.

Pray and ask God what needs to be reprioritized, or let go of it to get on God's path for your life today.

Blake

MATTHEW 6:33

(NLT)

> Seek the Kingdom of God above all else, and live righteously, and He will give you everything you need.

When I first became a Christian, I was living in a converted barn loft. It had a bed, heat, air, shower, toilet, washer, and dryer. I was allowed to stay there as long as I cared for my landlord's cattle. It was certainly a blessing, because I didn't have the money for a place of my own, and it allowed me pay down some debt. I was lacking a lot of things, and I didn't have the plans or ability to get my life straightened out.

The debt was on my mind a lot. One day while reading my Bible, I came across Matthew 6:33: "Seek the Kingdom of God above all else, and live righteously, and He will give you everything you need." In this verse and the ones before it, I was taught to focus on God, live righteously, and not be concerned with what I am going to eat, wear, or live. He promises to take care of our needs, and He has been faithful!

Twenty years later, I have a wonderful wife, kiddos, a home, and my dream job. Even now, there are times I try to take care of things on my own, and I have to remind myself to focus on God, who has always cared for me.

James

ACTS 1:11

(NIV)

> "Men of Galilee," they said, "why do you stand here looking into the sky? This same Jesus who has been taken from you into heaven, will come back in the same way you have seen him go into heaven."

One of the most exciting parts of bass fishing for me is the morning "blastoff"! Whether it's a tournament or just a fun day on the water, nothing beats the anticipation of getting out there. I remember so many times when I could hardly sleep the night before a day on the water. Thoughts of catching huge numbers of giant bass made me keep one eye on the clock, waking at every hour!

I always have to keep in mind that there is a lot to do before I get to that blastoff. There are batteries to charge, lines to tie, lures to choose, and hooks to sharpen. I must check to see that the motor is running, the lights work, the plug is in … the list goes on and on. I also need to make sure that I practice. Practicing casting and fishing enables me to become the angler I want to be.

In the book of Acts, Jesus is miraculously taken up into the clouds right before the very eyes of his disciples. As they stand dumbfounded, staring into the clouds, the Bible records that two men remind them that instead of staring in the clouds, they need to get some things done before Jesus returns. He tells them to go into all the world to preach the good news and to make disciples, and to teach them to obey everything He had commanded.

The day of His return, Jesus will be—in every sense of the word—awesome! Until that time, we need to be about doing the will of God in our lives. Do you know the will of God for your life? Are you doing it?

Chris

PSALM 18:28

(HCSB)

Lord, you light my lamp;
my God illuminates my darkness.

I have had some of the most awesome times fishing after dark. I even landed my personal-best largemouth, weighing close to fourteen pounds, off a dock in the middle of the night. It might be the lack of pressure after dark, or possibly the fish are just a little easier to trick with little to no light. Either way, if you can go out there safely, I highly encourage it.

If you have ever been on a lake after dark, you might agree that it's one of the most peaceful yet terrifying things you can ever experience. It's peaceful because you know no one else is out there with you, but also slightly nerve-racking for the exact same reason.

No matter where I go, Psalm 18:28 goes through my head because I know God illuminates my darkness—not only in the physical, but also the spiritual. When the Enemy attacks, darkness seems to surround me on all sides. The incredible thing is that because the Holy Spirit resides in me, He pushes back that darkness, filling my mind with truth, hope, and peace and strengthening me to carry on. Hallelujah that we serve a God that lights up our darkness, and He always will!

Let Christ shine on your darkness today, and try giving all your fears to Him.

Blake

PROVERBS 14:12

(N L T)

> There is a path before each person that seems right, but it ends in death.

It's amazing to me how often in life I am sure of a plan, a path forward, and then run in that direction wholeheartedly. In a BASS Elite Series event on the St. Johns River, I went on a forty-five-minute run to Lake George. I was fishing to the last minute when I saw a storm building in the distance, preceded by a squall line with wind and rain that quickly engulfed Lake George. The rain turned into a hard downpour, and I could barely see my GPS mapping because of the super heavy precipitation. Relying on my own sense of direction, I set out across the lake. Thinking I was almost to the other side, I wiped the water off my GPS screen only to have it reveal that I was heading in the wrong direction.

I was in such disbelief about my path being incorrect that I thought something was wrong with my GPS and made very little correction. In my mind, I was sure I knew where I was going and that it was the right way. Shortly, I saw a landmark that revealed that I was going the wrong way, and thankfully my actions didn't result in being late for the scheduled weigh-in time.

This life experience reminds me of how easy it can be for us to get off track while wholeheartedly believing that we have the right plan, path, or idea figured out when we are only relying on ourselves for direction or the choices we make. Thankfully, we have the Bible, which can be referenced like a GPS for making the best decisions about how to live and which path to take.

James

2 CORINTHIANS 5:17

(NLT)

> This means that anyone who belongs to Christ has become a new person. The old has gone, the new is here!

I grew up in a family that loved not only catching fish but eating them as well. Some of the best memories I have are of sitting at the table with my dad and uncles eating fish and grits as stories about how those fish were caught flew around the room like fireflies. I have found, however, that even though I enjoy catching and eating fish, I don't enjoy cleaning fish.

I cleaned my first fish for a merit badge back in Boy Scouts. I still remember the shock of what I saw and smelled as I cut that crappie open to get it ready to fry. To say I was a little "green" is an understatement. Eventually I came to realize that if I wanted to enjoy that great meal of fish, cleaning the fish was the essential first step.

This experience is not unlike what happens to us when Jesus transforms our lives. As He slides the dip net of his grace around us, he begins the process of cleaning. The cleaning is not like the external cleaning we do when we wash our truck or bathe our dog. It's more like what happens when we clean a fish. When the fish is laid bare, it exposes for all to see what is really on the inside. He slices open the dead and cuts away everything that is not needed into a form only He can use. That lifeless piece of protein is marvelously changed and becomes part of something much grander.

It's not easy to allow Jesus to change us, but that is exactly what needs to happen. Are you allowing Jesus to clean your life? Open it up to Him, and allow Him to do His work in making you something new!

Chris

MATTHEW 11:28

(HCSB)

> Come to me, all you who are weary and burdened,
> and I will give you rest.

There are literally no longer days of the year than those first couple days of summer that last about fifteen hours, especially on a northern lake. With most of those days ranging from fifteen to sixteen hours and set practice times from daylight to dark, you must give it everything you have to keep looking.

I'll never forget the time I had the flu and made a twenty-three-hour drive to get to one of those northern lakes. With long practice days, it was the perfect storm. I fished the tournament literally from my knees on the front of the boat.

In life, we find ourselves in similar situations, weary, burdened, and broken mentally and physically. This world has a way of tearing us down. However, isn't it refreshing to know we serve a God who gives us rest when we ask for it? The circumstances may not change, but God is the God of Peace, and if we lean into Him and surrender what is consuming us, His presence will overwhelm us. He will empower us with a strength that is not our own and give us peace that no one can make sense of.

God is good like that. He makes it very simple. The key is His saying, "Come to Me." So take the first step, talk to Him, and lay it all at His feet. He is big enough to handle it—His Word says so.

Try resting in Him today. Lay your struggles and the things consuming you at His feet.

Blake

ROMANS 1:20

(NLT)

> For ever since the world was created, people have seen the earth and sky. Through everything God made, they can clearly see his invisible qualities—his eternal power and divine nature. So they have no excuse for not knowing God.

It is simply amazing how you can look out across the ocean, up to a high mountain peak, or from a lookout point and be captivated by what is before you. Sometimes in these moments when I witness God's creation, it almost makes me short of breath—it becomes clear how small I am, and how amazing God is to have created such beauty. From an early age, I've always looked forward to getting away from the city and spending time alone or with family in the outdoors.

That's why Romans 1:20 really resonated with me from the first time I heard it. I'm truly blessed to fish for a living, and while some of the long drives can be quite laborious, towing my boat from location to location allows me to see so many states. While some are prettier than others, I like to look for and appreciate the beauty of each area, which I feel is a reflection of our Creator, God. I truly don't know how anyone can look at all of God's glorious creation and believe that it got here by accident.

Jesus would get away into the wilderness to be alone and pray (Luke 5:16), so let's follow His example. Remove the distractions, and take in the scenery, so we can be reminded by what God spoke into being.

James

1 JOHN 1:9

(K J V)

> If we confess our sins, He is faithful and just to forgive us our sins, and cleanse us from all unrighteousness.

One night, I was sharing a fishing yarn with a couple of very bright fishing prodigies who were both eager to learn what I knew about catching bass. The more they listened, the more I got into the story! I was sharing about a time when I boated a sizable largemouth on my favorite crank bait. As I lectured, I took the lure out of my tackle box and began to use it as a visual aid. When I arrived at the pinnacle of the story, the part where I told them I got hooked, I slammed the lure I was holding down into my hand. You guessed it. I got hooked again! I spent a couple hours in the emergency room, listening to the cackles of every doctor and nurse who joked about the biggest one I ever caught. It was a storytelling mistake that was humiliating, to say the least. I wanted to slip out and hide.

Sin makes us do just that. We want to run out and hide. And oftentimes that is exactly what people do when they make mistakes. We hide them, cover them up, and evade them at every turn. What we should do is take them to the emergency room of the New Testament.

First John 1:9 says, "If we confess our sins, He is faithful to forgive us our sins and cleanse us from all unrighteousness." To *confess* means to come to an agreement or partnership with God in which we turn to Him and acknowledge that He is right and we are wrong. When we do that, God is faithful to do His part.

What sins are you hiding? Confess your sins to Him today.

Chris

ROMANS 12:2

(NIV)

> Do not conform to the pattern of this world but be transformed by the renewing of your mind. Then you will be able to test and approve what God's will is—His good, pleasing, and perfect will.

Too many times, I have let "dock talk" pull me in and lead me to do what everyone else was doing. But some of the best tournaments in my life were the ones when I did something completely different from the rest of the anglers. Sometimes acting on your preferences and strengths will lead to a ton more fishing success in the long run.

It's not hard to find ourselves going with the flow of the world we live in. Sometimes it seems easier to conform and do what everyone else is doing. Many days in my testimony-building years, I found myself doing exactly that—conforming. The world tells you that it's OK to have just one sip, or a relationship with that person, or even that just one look won't hurt you. In actuality, every one of those things is drawing you further from the Truth. We must be able to identify whether they fall into God's plan for our life or not.

We are called to be set apart from the world. Live differently. Live transformed. How do we do that? Well, He says, by the renewing of your mind. If you're not spending time in the Bible, God's Holy alive and active Word, you will be ill equipped to change. You will lack the connection to His voice, the Holy Spirit, who convicts us and gives us power and a way out of the temptations we face daily.

Try breaking away from the pack today, and live differently—the way God is calling you to live. Swim against the current!

Blake

PHILIPPIANS 4:8

(NLT)

> And now, dear brothers and sisters, one final thing. Fix your thoughts on what is true, and honorable, and right, and pure, and lovely, and admirable. Think about things that are excellent and worthy of praise.

Philippians 4:8 is a great scripture to help us deal with the changes and challenges of life. I am so blessed to be able to live out my lifelong dream of fishing for a living. Being a professional bass fisherman can be incredible, but it can also really challenge your mental toughness during a roller-coaster day—or a roller-coaster season.

My wife has been instrumental in getting this scripture to into our kids' heads and keeping a proper perspective on life, and it has been very helpful for me. This scripture is such a reminder of what we are to do when we are bombarded with thoughts, some of which are our very own and yet counterproductive for what we are working towards. A lost fish first thing in the morning could be detrimental to the day's productivity if I stew on it and replay that scenario over in my head, but it is at that moment that I must be my own coach and "fix my thoughts" on what is "excellent and worthy of praise." In the heat of the game, I have to be my own coach, and God's Word gives me the answer on how to do that.

Philippians 4:8 is helpful for steering away from that mental snowball effect or downward spiral when disappointments happen. One thing is for sure: life does have it's peaks and valleys, so whenever they come our way, it's important refer to this scripture, to fix our thoughts "on what is true, and honorable, and right, and pure, and lovely, and admirable." Thinking about things that are "excellent and worthy of praise."

James

JAMES 1:22

(ESV)

> Be doers of the Word and not hearers only, deceiving yourselves.

The exponential growth of fishing information and knowledge over the years has been immense. Television shows, internet videos, magazines, books, seminars, and fishing expos have all provided boundless information on the how-tos of fishing. The years it used to take to accumulate and learn through trial and error can now be bypassed in a fraction of the time. A good student of fishing can learn about tying knots, finding fish, and the best lures along with acquiring the essential tools.

The only thing there's no shortcut for is putting that knowledge into practice. That must be *done*, not just learned. Many in the sport of fishing are great at hearing about fishing, collecting a vast array of the best lures, having the best equipment, and yet are never able to translate all that to actually catching fish. There is a vast difference in knowing about fishing and actually being able to catch fish.

The book of James talks about the difference in knowing what to do and actually doing it. James enlightens us to the fact that it's not enough to be a hearer of the Word of God—we must be doers. Many people today are content that they know all about the Word of God. They read about it, write about it, and can even quote it, but in fact they don't live it with their lives. The Bible says they are deceiving themselves about where they are. We aren't justified by what we do, but we do because we have been justified.

James says that if we are really born of God, it will show in how we live, not just in what we say. It's not enough to just sit in church and listen to what a preacher says. We must be active participants in the will of God for our lives.

Are you living what you say you believe? What adjustments do you need to make today?

Chris

MATTHEW 5:9

(N I V)

> Blessed are the peacekeepers, for they will be called children of God.

In fishing competitively, as in any sport, you're going to find yourself at odds with your competitors. In most situations, you are each competing for the same prize, the same fish, and many of the same spots to fish in. The higher I have climbed in the game, the easier it is to see that most of us are thinking the same things at the same time and will end up in the exact same spots throughout the day. Believe me, after a time, this will lead to a run-in.

As important as it is to remain competitive throughout the day, we are called to peace first. I have developed a philosophy over the years on and off the water: "If they can live with it, I can live without it." Having a turn-the-other-cheek mentality sounds easier than it really is, but God shows us in His word how important that is as a follower of Christ. Being at peace with others was a crucial part of Jesus's ministry here on earth, and also a vital part of the lessons set out for us in the Sermon on the Mount. Without peace, we have zero ability to have relationships with others, and without relationships with others, we have zero ability to fulfill the calling God has for each of us to be fishers of men.

So I guess you could say the more at peace we are with the people around us, the more opportunity we will have to minister to others and be the reflection of Christ Himself.

Try and be at peace with those around you today.

Blake

COLOSSIANS 3:13

(NLT)

> Make allowance for each other's faults, and forgive anyone who offends you. Remember, the Lord forgave you, so you must forgive others.

In any sport, it is just a matter of time before some type of conflict arises between competitors. When the desire to excel and accomplish something is met with opposition, during the heat of competition sparks tend to fly.

Conflicts on the water are not as common as some might think they are, but how we as professionals handle conflicts is important to the companies we represent. Similarly it's very important to us as Christians. How we represent Christ in the workplace, on the water, or on the road is important—and Colossians 3:13 tells us how to do just that.

During a Bassmaster Elite Series event on the second day of one particular tournament, I had a conflict with a friend and fellow competitor. A Bassmaster Classic qualification was on the line, and things weren't going well. I felt like the on-the-water friction between us was putting strain on our friendship. It wasn't about who was at fault. At the end of the day, I can only be responsible for my actions, and how I handled it bothered me. So once competition was over, I looked for him and apologized for the way I handled things. He forgave me, and today we still have a great friendship.

Relationships are valuable, and we should be good stewards of each one that God gives us. At one time or another, we all need to forgive or be forgiven, and Colossians 3:13 encourages us to follow the Lord's example.

James

HEBREWS 11:1

(K J V)

> Now faith is the substance of things hoped for,
> the evidence of things not seen.

A good friend of mine was teaching his daughter how to fish. She was very young, and they proceeded to head down to a local pond to see if the bluegills were biting. He pointed to a spot that looked good and told her that this was where they should fish.

"How do you know the fish are there, Daddy?" his daughter asked.

"You have to have faith that they are there," my friend answered.

There is a great lesson for us in this. It's been said that fishing is like playing a round of golf with your eyes blindfolded. You can't always see the goal. You have to have faith that the fish are where you are casting your lures. The core of fishing is faith, just as Christianity hinges upon faith. The writer of Hebrews goes on to say, "And without faith it is impossible to please God, because anyone who comes to him must believe that he exists and that he rewards those who earnestly seek him" (11:6 NIV).

Trusting God means trusting with your heart, soul, mind, and being. Not just trusting your eyes. It's not easy to trust something you can't see, but that is exactly what He asks us to do.

Have you placed your faith in Him? What hinders you from doing that right now?

Chris

MARK 9:23

(HCSB)

> Then Jesus said to him, "'If You can'? Everything is possible to the one who believes."

As strong as I feel my faith is, I find myself time and time again throughout the year trying to force situations, owing to my lack of faith. The concept of only needing faith the size of a mustard seed giving you mountain moving power keeps me in check with the reality that I can always use more faith.

After the last cast each year, most pros in the industry spend countless hours working on securing the sponsorship to compete in the next season. Many of us find ourselves in the beginning of our careers wondering if it will all come together—wondering if all the ends will meet again, and the next season will remain possible. This situation gets a ton easier every year, but early on can leave you slightly nervous. I remember Meagan, my wife, always saying if God wants you there, He will always provide, and He always has.

We don't have to question God in His motives—only our own. Jesus's response to a question of disbelief in Mark 9:23 remains true for us today. These men were face to face with Jesus and still doubted. One of His disciples was even nicknamed Doubting Thomas, so it's easy to see how we can fall into the same trap centuries later. "Everything is possible to the one who believes" was true two thousand years ago and is just as powerful today. If we believe, truly believe, and don't lack faith, we can see those mountains move.

Try to live out your faith today—not just through your words, but through your actions.

Blake

JOSHUA 1:9

(ESV)

> Have I not commanded you? Be strong and courageous. Do not be frightened, and do not be dismayed, for the Lord your God is with you wherever you go.

I would not describe myself as a person who is fearful or afraid, and most people may think the same of themselves. However, day in and day out, I do gravitate towards things that are *probable*.

In tournament fishing, I like to work with the percentages and make decisions that lead to a higher likelihood of success. What qualifies as success may vary, depending on how practice went, or for a multiday tournament, how things went the day before. Competition at the tour level depends on making cuts to advance to the next round, and I will naturally make decisions that should lead me to making the cut. Making cuts means getting paid, and that is always good; however, the cut line is generally a fair way off the pace from qualifying for the finals. Making a choice to aim for the top ten requires being stronger and operating more courageously. You have to try for a better grade of fish, and that isn't as "safe" as targeting the larger population of smaller fish on a given fishery.

In life as in tournament fishing, you have to find a balance and know when to push things. But wherever we are, or whatever we are faced with, God is asking us to be courageous and strong. Remember, God *commands* us to be strong and courageous, and there is a greater degree of productivity in that than in shrinking back. I've learned over the years that when I have operated from a place of being frightened or dismayed, I have generally missed out on something more that God had for me. So push through, press on, and choose to stir up strength and courage with in you.

James

MATTHEW 4:19

(E S V)

And He said to them, "Follow me, and I will make you fishers of men."

There are very few things in life that spur the imagination of a fisherman more than a warm morning in the early spring when bass move shallow to spawn. During this time, the chances of catching a big bass increase exponentially. The visual experience that bedding fish present to an angler has no equal.

The techniques used to corral these fish are varied, and although exciting, it is not always easy. Some days, fishing for bedding fish can be an exercise in absolute frustration. I've seen times when it seems you can throw your entire tackle box, and the fish just will not bite. When that happens, the temptation is to give up on the fish and just move on. However, I've learned from watching many bass pros that perseverance pays off.

There can be several reasons that fish won't bite. It could be that a change in color, presentation, line size, or distance will help the problem. And while sometimes one change makes the difference, it could just be plain repetition—often, the persistent angler can catch that fish.

Many times as Christians we have trouble with evangelism. We share the gospel with a friend or family member, and if they don't come to faith immediately, we give up. There are several things we need to remember. First of all, God does the saving. None of us can save anyone. Second, we are successful when we simply share the good news in a way that honors Christ. Sharing with humility and kindness can be the key. And third, patience and persistence pay off.

So don't give up. It can pay off with the catch of an eternity!

Chris

PHILIPPIANS 4:13

(HCSB)

> I am able to do all things through Him who strengthens me.

Nine times a year, I find myself in a seemingly impossible situation, up against seemingly impossible odds. Fishing that many times every year against one hundred and sixty of the best anglers in the world can really seem impossible. I'm not doubting my God-given abilities to catch fish, but these guys are just that good—not to mention that my best days on tour would fall somewhere below the Mendoza line of professional baseball.[1] However, I can have confidence that even though the learning curve through the intricacies of the game is as hard as it is, there is nothing we can't do, and I can do all things through Him who gives me strength.

While in prison, Paul wrote in Philippians about how we are more than capable of handling whatever the world throws at us. As someone with firsthand knowledge of true struggle and plenty of reasons to feel like throwing in the towel, Paul explained what perseverance in Christ looks like in life. He illustrated that through good times and bad, there are no circumstances that don't pass through God's hands first. We must remember where our strength comes from and face our difficulties with the confidence that only comes from trusting God with everything.

What impossible odds do you find yourself facing?

Blake

---

[1] The "Mendoza line" is a standard of minimum competence, named for shortstop Mario Mendoza, whose batting average stayed below .200 in five of his nine seasons of Major League Baseball.

COLOSSIANS 3:23

(NIV)

Whatever you do, work at it with all your heart,
as working for the Lord, not for human masters.

When I was a new Christian, I was working at a tackle store and doing some guide trips on Lake Fork on the side. If I am honest, I didn't have the greatest of work habits, but I remember either reading or hearing a scripture that changed how I thought about work: "Whatever you do, work at it with all your heart, as working for the Lord, not human masters." Back then, it was surprising to me that God's Word would speak to us about how we should conduct ourselves in the workplace. Then I recognized that because I had surrendered all of myself to the Lordship of Jesus Christ, even my work ethic, and how I applied myself to the smallest of remedial jobs, really mattered.

Reading Colossians 3:23 along with Luke 16:10 (NIV)—"Whoever can be trusted with very little can also be trusted with much, and whoever is dishonest with very little will also be dishonest with much"—was convicting and eye-opening about how as a follower of Jesus I needed to work on my perspective.

It's funny as I look back now, because I don't know why it wasn't obvious to me that working hard for your employer, whoever that may be, can only get you noticed and poised for a promotion. In the eyes of the world, giving more might not seem smart, because if you're going to get paid the same either way, why not just deliver what's been asked of you and nothing more? But in God's kingdom, we are to follow Jesus's example to serve and be a blessing to those around us. Doing so could give us the opportunity to share what makes us different, and if asked we can answer only "Jesus!"

James

JOHN 16:3

(E S V)

> When the Spirit of truth comes, he will guide you into all the truth. For he will not speak on his own, but he will speak whatever he hears. He will also declare to you what is to come.

Several years ago, I took a student of mine fishing on Lake Hartwell in South Carolina. It was a cool day, and a heavy fog had enveloped the lake in a thick haze that was hard to see through. We persevered and climbed into the boat, excited about spending a day fishing. I was experienced in navigating the lake, and despite the fog I thought I could get us to the spot we needed to go.

We idled out and passed a small sandbar that had a flag stuck in it. I kept the flag to my left, pointed the boat in the direction I thought was straight, and kept going. Twenty minutes later, I passed the same sandbar with the flag. After repeating this circuit three times that morning, we decided to stay put until the fog cleared.

I thought we were heading straight where we needed to go, but as it turns out, I was only making a giant circle. I needed a reliable guide to help me that day. These days, boats have GPS units on them. Global positioning systems can help you know you are navigating correctly even when your eyes deceive you.

In the Christian life, our guide is the Holy Spirit. The Holy Spirit is God living inside us. The Bible tells us that He will guide us into all truth. He convicts, rebukes, corrects, and empowers us to live the Christian life. Every true follower of Christ has the power of the Holy Spirit available in their lives. The problem is that too often we try to rely on our own power.

Do you hear the voice of the Holy Spirit in your life? Do you depend upon His guidance or your own? Yield to Him today.

Chris

HEBREWS 13:5

(NIV)

> Keep your lives free from the love of money and be content with what you have.

There have been times in my life when I felt like I couldn't get enough. I thought I needed the best truck, the nicest boat, all the top equipment, vacations, clothes ... the list goes on and on. As high up the ladder as I felt that I was climbing, I was in fact in a downward spiral, destined for destruction. The drive to acquire possessions had consumed me, and a lack of contentment was tearing me apart from the inside. I am so thankful that it was just a season in my life and not a road I continued on.

The world tells us to be driven by consumption and the desire for more, but that is a terrible path to follow. Here is the truth: it's not God's desire for us to acquire so many things that we stop asking for His provision and favor. We are called to be in constant communion with God, and the more we crave the power of money, the less we desire God as our source. Everything we have is from Him and through Him.

I remember very clearly believing the lie from the Enemy that I was the one making everything happen. I made money my god and didn't even realize it. I worshipped it, idolized it, and even found myself living for it. Unfortunately, I was missing the contentment that comes from a relationship with Christ.

Do you ever find yourself craving things that pull you farther from God? It's not too late to realign your heart and love.

Blake

GALATIANS 6:4–6

(NLT)

> Pay careful attention to your own work, for then you will get the satisfaction of a job well done, and you won't need to compare yourself to anyone else. For we are each responsible for your own conduct.

In professional tournament bass fishing, it can be really difficult to keep your head down, work hard, look over, and not have thoughts of comparing yourself to someone else. Like any other sport, tournament fishing is highly competitive, and what dictates where you finish at the end each day is, after all, a comparison of your catches with the competition's.

It doesn't end there, though, because only a finite number of sponsorships are available within the fishing industry. Who lands what from each company is based on a comparison of your tournament finishes, how well you can promote yourself for each company, and how visible you are to the fishing world at large. Your competition is vying for each dollar available to be earned both on and off the water.

So it may be difficult to do your own work well without measuring it against what others do, but it's not impossible if you apply the valuable advice from Galatians 6:4–6: "Pay careful attention to your own work, for then you will get the satisfaction of a job well done, and you won't need to compare yourself to anyone else. For we are each responsible for our own conduct."

I have been told that even when you have a difficult day on the water, you don't have to feel bad about it if you've given it your all. If you've done your best, you can still get satisfaction from your efforts. You may want to have a higher finish or an event win, but you can only control your own performance on the water, and just as important as the outcome or results is how you conduct yourself afterwards. But in my opinion, there is another perspective from which to look at the competitive side of tournament fishing, as well as at other things in life, and it lines up well with this scripture. Do your best to apply yourself so you can have a good day, and should things go well, it really doesn't matter who your competition is, because there isn't anyone who can take that away from you.

So I encourage you to apply Galatians 6:4–6 to your life. It will give you the satisfaction of giving everything your best, and there really isn't anything more that anyone can ask of you.

James

HEBREWS 10:24–25

(NIV)

> And let us consider how we may spur one another on toward love and good deeds, not giving up meeting together, as some are in the habit of doing, but let us encourage one another—and all the more as you see the Day approaching.

Most of my heroes growing up were bass pros! I am not kidding. Guys might come up to me and say, "Chris, did you see what Terry Bradshaw did on the football field today?" and my reply would be, "Never mind Terry Bradshaw. Did you see what Hank Parker caught today? He must have caught thirty pounds!" I am totally enamored with the sport of bass fishing.

Roland Martin, Bill Dance, Jimmy Houston, Hank Parker, Shaw Grigsby, Al Lindner, Orlando Wilson ... I love them all. I once startled everyone in the house by jumping over my couch in a frenzy, grabbing the remote to desperately catch the last fifteen minutes of a bass fishing show. I'm "hooked"!

But you know what? As much as I love to watch fishing shows, there is nothing like getting to know those guys personally. I have been blessed by getting to spend time with some of the greatest fishermen in the world, and it always makes me want to be a better fisherman. The fellowship and interaction makes the relationships that much richer.

I meet a lot of men today who talk a lot about God but strangely don't ever go to church. They may listen to a preacher on the radio, read a book, or maybe even watch a service on television, and while there's nothing wrong with that, it's essential for a man to physically *be* in a church. That's because the Church, capital C, is not just a building—it's a living, breathing entity. It's a body of believers who are literally the bride of Christ Himself. When we are present with one another to worship, pray, encourage, and fellowship together, it creates something as believers we simply cannot live without. Hebrews tells us not to forsake the assembling of ourselves together.

Have you found yourself making excuses about why you are not going to church? Make it a point right now to get back there this Sunday.

Chris

PSALM 73:26

(NIV)

> My flesh and heart may fail, but God is the strength of my heart and my portion forever.

If you ever want a preview of what it means to have your flesh fail, fish professionally for a few years. Taking a beating from waves, lacking sleep, spending days on your feet, driving cross-country while consuming way too much caffeine ... I know you're sitting there thinking, *I hope he's not complaining about fishing for a living.* I assure you, I would never complain about the best job on the planet! But the strain this career puts on your body does wear on you.

Every morning before getting up, I pray for God to grant me a perseverance that can only come from Him. It's those days when I get up tired and beaten down that I most remember what my purpose is and why my family and I are on this journey to glorify God and tell the good news of His Son, Jesus.

How exciting is it to know that no matter what I put my body through on earth while doing His will, He is my strength and portion forever. One day this flesh will undoubtedly fail, but I will give it everything I have until then, and there is nothing that pushes you more or keeps you as encouraged as doing the will of God.

Ask God today for the strength to be everything He needs you to be today.

Blake

HEBREWS 12:1–3

(NIV)

> Let us run with perseverance the race marked out for us, fixing our eyes on Jesus, the pioneer and perfecter of faith, who for the joy set before him endured the cross, scorning its shame, and sat down at the right hand of God. Consider Him who endured such opposition from sinners, so that you will not grow weary and lose heart.

In life, the list of dreams, aspirations, and goals seems to be never-ending. Whether it is catching a ten-pound bass, advancing to the next level of competition wherever you compete, or getting in better shape, we all have to set goals and focus our aim so we can make that dream a reality. In the same way, it is important to be purposeful about our Christian walk and to have a plan for how we are going to pursue our relationship with Jesus.

Hebrews 12:2 tells us to fix our eyes on Jesus so that we don't grow weary and lose heart. Something that has really helped me fix my eyes on Jesus more consistently is the YouVersion Bible App. It has a daily scripture and various devotionals so I can prioritize my time each morning with scripture, and that has been super helpful in directing my day, my heart, and my mind. It takes a degree of discipline to follow, but there will always be a sacrifice of time and effort to make anything worth pursuing happen.

I've heard it said that any boat without a rudder or power source to actively move it in a particular direction has the potential to drift away from its intended destination. Quiet time alone with God in prayer or in His Word helps build our faith and keep our rudder straight. As Hebrews 12:2 encourages us, we must keep our attention fixed on Jesus if we are not to grow weary and lose heart.

James

1 JOHN 1:7

(NIV)

> If we walk in the Light as He is in the light, we have fellowship with one another, and the blood of Jesus His Son purifies us from all sin.

Quite a number of years ago, my uncle decided to take up a new hobby: bow fishing. He got a giant aluminum boat and decked it out with about ten high-powered spotlights. A generator was mounted on the boat to provide the power, and the results were incredible. He could go out on the water on a dark moonless night and illuminate things that we had no idea were there! You could see absolutely everything. Fish we never knew existed were exposed for all to see, because that is what light does. It exposes.

First John 1:5 tells that "God is light. In Him there is no darkness at all," and verse 6 goes on to say that if we claim to have fellowship or walk with Him but still are walking in darkness, that cannot be. We are not being truthful with God or ourselves. We need to expose it. Let it walk in the light.

Now, to walk in the light does not mean that we walk 100 percent without sin. It does mean, however, that we bring that sin into the light of God. That is the only way for a man to truly have peace and fellowship with the Father.

So how do we do that? You know this already: you confess your sin to Him. Bring it into the light. God can handle it. It is not easy for a man to truly confess what he has done wrong, but it is the only way to be freed from it.

What darkness is in your life today that needs to be brought into the light?

Chris

ROMANS 8:39

(N I V)

> Neither height nor depth, nor anything else in all creation will be able to separate us from the love of God that is in Christ Jesus our Lord.

Pickwick Lake, 2016. Everything was going as planned on day one. I ran from takeoff up to Lake Wilson, locked through, and caught everything I needed to have a successful day. I returned to the locks hours before I had to be back for weigh in—and that's when everything went downhill.

A barge was stuck, and thirty-two other pros and I found ourselves locked outside the locks, resulting in our returning to weigh in three hours late and a disqualification for the day. Nothing worries you more as a tournament angler on the water than not making it to weigh in, and there are a ton of factors that can keep you from getting there. But as Christians, we can have peace in knowing that nothing can separate us from the love of God. No matter what obstacles we face or what sins we have committed, nothing can keep us from the agape love of our Creator through His Son Jesus.

When Jesus gave His life for us on the cross, and the curtain was torn from top to bottom, we were assured that nothing could separate us from the Father. We can go straight to Him personally to hand Him all our cares and concerns. There are literally no circumstances we can find ourselves in that are too far gone or too deep for our Savior to pull us out of.

Try casting all your cares upon Him today, and experience the communion with your Creator.

Blake

MATTHEW 7:24

(NLT)

> Anyone who listens to my teaching and follows it is wise, like a person who builds a house on solid rock.

Life is certainly interesting. How we navigate through life with the choices we make can affect how things go for us. If someone is not a Christian, the ideas and ways in which they make decisions may change from one day to the next, based on how well a particular situation suits them. As Christians, we adopt a biblical world view that we reference so that we make good choices that line up with God's will for us, because we recognize that God's way is higher than our own.

Sometimes I have a tendency to have "fishing brain"—I try to apply God's Word and important life lessons to fishing. For every tour-level fishing event, we have two to three days of official practice for scouting the tournament waters, or what we call "practicing." This is an important time so that when the tournament starts, we have identified fish holding areas and what the fish are doing. During this time, we may catch a fish that fits with what we believe to be the proper seasonal pattern that the fish may be in for the given time we are there. This fish, the area, the bait we used can lead us to think that what we've found has real potential, but we can invest a lot of time chasing something that goes away—or worse, has no substance. Because we misidentified what stage or seasonal pattern most of the fish are in, we began our search on a faulty foundation.

Even in fishing it's important to make wise choices based on what is truly happening, so that you can build on it and go the distance for multiple days. We can have full confidence that God's Word is a firm foundation or "solid rock" on which to build our lives, both now and into eternity.

James

LAMENTATIONS 3:22–23

(NIV)

Because of the Lord's great love, we are not consumed,
for his compassions never fail.
They are new every morning;
great is your faithfulness.

There are times when tournament bass fishing can be quite frustrating. I fished a tournament once where from the moment we put the boat in the water, everything went wrong. The boat cranked perfectly at the start, but when I went to turn the steering wheel, it was locked up completely. Since we could not turn, we decided to fish with only the trolling motor. During the day, the trolling motor shorted out and would allow us only to turn right, so we had to compete with no big motor and making only right turns!

A bad tournament can make even the most exuberant angler want to put his rods and reels up for sale and take up another hobby. There are days when the fish just don't bite, the boat breaks down, the bass jumps off, and every decision seems like the wrong one. Life can be just like that. There will be days even in the life of the believer when we want to throw our hands up and just give up.

The good thing about fishing days and the Christian life is that every day is a fresh start. Each day we get to start again with a clean slate. The Bible tells us that the mercies of God are new each morning, and that is a promise worth hearing again and again.

Do you need a fresh start? If *yes* is the answer that came to your mind, then go to God with that today. His mercies are brand-new.

Chris

MATTHEW 14:27–29

(HCSB)

Jesus spoke to them. "Have courage! It is I, don't be afraid."

"Lord, if it's You," Peter answered Him, "Command me to come to you on the water."

"Come!" He said.

It doesn't matter how many miracles I've seen in my life; I still find myself asking God for courage to face certain situations. It's almost as if I need a continued affirmation that He is still right there holding my hand no matter what life circumstances I find myself in. I'll never forget when I was called into missions and full-time tour ministry. It was such a confusing time of second-guessing myself about every life decision I was making. Every door was opening, and God made all the provisions, and yet I still found myself asking for one more sign or maybe a bigger sign.

Peter knew Jesus personally, walked with Him, and still had to muster up enough faith to step out of the boat when Jesus called him. By walking with God and staying in close communion with Him, we increase our ability to identify His voice and have the confidence to step out of the boat when called to do so.

God has already told us not to be afraid and that He will go with us wherever we go, so what are we waiting for? Would you recognize His voice if He called, and are you ready to step out of the boat when He does?

Blake

ROMANS 3:22–24

(NLT)

> We are made right with God by placing our faith in Jesus Christ. And this is true for everyone who believes, no matter who we are. For everyone has sinned; we all fall short of God's glorious standard. Yet God, with undeserved kindness, declares that we are righteous.

When I read Romans 3:22, I am reminded of the day that I surrendered my life to Jesus Christ. I remember most of what happened that day: where I was, who was there, and how it happened. I didn't fully grasp the magnitude of how special the day was. I was a new creation in Christ, and I was restored back to right relationship to the very One who created my soul. It was that day when I would begin to know Jesus as my Lord and Savior.

This scripture reminds me how truly amazing God's character is. The day I trusted Christ, I was living life my way and not thinking much, if at all, about God's ways; but in that moment, as soon as I turned to Him, He accepted me. The scriptures say that no matter who we are, we are made right with God when we place our faith in Jesus Christ. Even in our sinfulness, God has mercy for each one of us. He gives us that amazing "undeserved kindness." Now that is love!

I had to ask myself how often I give someone underserved kindness. How about you? You may show undeserved kindness to your immediate family or friends, but even now, I find that sadly it is not something that I regularly show others. It is even more of a struggle to forgive someone who has wronged you, but we've all sinned and fallen short of God's glorious standard, and God still declares us righteous. We truly serve a loving God!

Today, take some time to think about how loving, kind, and merciful God is.

James

HEBREWS 8:12

(CSB)

> For I will forgive their wrongdoing, and I will never again remember their sins.

Quite a few years ago, the braided line started to make its way back into the fishing market. It is an effective tool that has several fantastic applications. Some of its advantages include getting big fish out of thick cover, as well as obtaining solid hook sets on very long casts because it has zero stretch. The old monofilament line is known for turning your bait cast reel into a prominent "bird nest." Not so with braid. I love braid because it has no memory whatsoever and does not remember your casting mistakes.

As a father, a husband, or even as a child, each of us has committed sins or mistakes in life that that we wish we could forget—things we wish we could take back or just banish from our consciousness forever. Regrets we have that seem to never go away.

The Bible tells us that God has the ability to do just that. When he forgives us, he can choose never to remember our sins again. The book of Psalms says he can cast our sins as far as the east is to the west! He makes our lives brand-new. He truly is an awesome God!

What sins do you need for God never to remember again? Take those to him and leave them today.

Chris

COLOSSIANS 3:2

(HCSB)

> Set your minds on what is above, and not on what
> is on the earth.

I will never forget the day I stopped stressing the fish. I was fishing Guntersville in Alabama, and a good friend of mine, Mark Rose, gave me some words of encouragement after a terrible practice. He said, "Blake, whether you catch them or not, it doesn't matter, because there is no eternal significance other than what you do for the Lord." That statement really stuck with me, not only because Mark went on to win that event and the following event, but because it changed my mindset forever.

Fast forward six years. As I was walking off the stage at the Forrest Wood Cup after receiving the Forrest L. Wood Sportsmanship and Community Service Award, I was stopped by Hank Parker. He said, "Blake, that award is awesome, but what you did for the Lord to earn that award will have an impact for eternity."

What I've learned in my career is that if I am so wrapped up in what's going on around me and all the things associated with life's everyday struggles, I am going to completely miss what God has set out for me in the long run. Set your mind to the things above, and watch the floodgates open. Let me make a disclaimer: I'm not saying you're going to win back-to-back tournaments like Mark did, but you might see a divine appointment open right before your eyes.

Try setting your mind to what is above today, and see what God has in store for you.

Blake

2 CORINTHIANS 9:7

(NIV)

> Each of you should give what you have decided in your heart to give, not reluctantly or under compulsion, for God loves a cheerful giver.

One of the most important faith-builders happened to me shortly after I became a Christian. I was at church one Sunday morning, and the pastor's message was on tithing. He said it is not popular for pastors to preach on tithing, but he challenged the congregation with a message on the importance of this biblical principal. As I recall, the pastor compelled us to begin tithing by giving 10 percent of our earnings back to the church, if we hadn't been doing that already. He said that God is a good provider and we should trust Him for our needs. He said to give God six months to show Himself faithful, and if after six months things weren't better, then go back to the way you did things before. He said that if we honored God with our finances, we would live better with 90 percent of our income with God than having 100 percent of it without God.

His message inspired me to start tithing, which I had never done before—and honestly, I didn't know if it was possible for me to do. Back then, I was living paycheck to paycheck, with a mountain of debt and a boat payment, and it didn't seem I would be able to set aside 10 percent to give back to God. Surrendering my finances to the Lord did take a leap of faith, but I did it, and I was able to see God quickly show Himself faithful.

God became even more personal to me in a short amount of time. I received an unsolicited raise at the tackle store where I worked, won some big bass money in a couple of tournaments, and began picking up some extra guide trips. It was amazing faith-builder for me to see God move in my life, and because I trusted Him with my money, I began trusting God in a greater way. Certainly, it did not mean that I would never face another financial challenge, but through it I knew I could trust God. He has always remained faithful to provide for me and now even more for the needs of our family.

James

2 CORINTHIANS 5:17

(NIV)

> Therefore, if anyone is in Christ, the new creation
> has come: The old has gone, the new is here!

Any fisherman will tell you that when you see a pile of old plastic worms—or any baits, for that matter—it was a good day fishing. The more plastics piled up in the bottom of the boat, the better. The vast majority of those baits are cast into the trash, never to be seen again. Some get reused as children's bath toys, and others are cast into the parking lot of boat ramps around the country. By and large, after they are fished, their usefulness is over.

A number of years back, a good friend of mine decided to try something new. He went and purchased a soft plastic set of fishing bait molds. He would melt down his old soft plastics and create brand-new fishing baits. Essentially he took something that was old, no good, and discarded and repurposed it to be brand-new.

In His Word, God says that is exactly what He does with us. He takes the old us and makes us brand-new. He gives us a new life, a new heart, a new mind, and a new purpose. He makes all things new. He did this when He spoke to our hearts, convicted us of sin, and called to us. We responded in faith and repentance, turning from sin and towards God.

The Bible says that this process of becoming new is so radical, it's like being born again! No matter how useless, downtrodden, sinful, and discarded we may be, God can make us new.

Thank God today that he just didn't discard you and cast you out. He redeemed you and made you new.

Chris

EPHESIANS 5:14

(HCSB)

Get up, sleeper, and rise from the dead,
and the Messiah will shine on you.

On tour, my alarm clock goes off at around four every morning. There are days when I want to turn it off and sleep for a few more hours and just let the day happen without me. The schedules and demands we have put on us throughout the year wear on us physically and mentally.

Admittedly, there are also many days throughout the year when I want to sleep in spiritually. As Christians, we're going to get beat up and abused by this world, and sometimes we may want nothing more than a day off or a time to just quit fighting. Add in the constant pressures of the world trying to block everything you were called to do for the Lord, and you have the perfect storm.

Thankfully, the Word of God gives us encouragement to wake up and fight because the Messiah has our back. Paul more than likely wrote Ephesians 5 as an encouragement to a non-Christian person living a life not devoted to Christ to wake up and turn to Him. However, it has always been a very encouraging verse to me not to live an idle life in my pursuit of my own sanctification. There is a constant battle going on around us, and it's going to take every single one of us to fight.

Today fight with confidence, because there is no better encouragement than knowing you're fighting a battle you're going to win.

Are you awake yet today? Get up and get ready for battle!

Blake

1 THESSALONIANS 5:18

(N L T)

> Be thankful in all circumstances, for this is God's
> will for you who belong to Christ Jesus.

Through the years of my Christian faith, I've come to recognize how much God desires good things for us. It is so evident in the scriptures. When I say "good things," I am not referring to what we might call "stuff" but to a life that is fruitful and a blessing to both you and those around you. Through this scripture, God is communicating how we should live. It is His will that things go well for you, while conversely the Enemy's desire is to steal, kill, and destroy all the good in your life.

Applying a heart of thankfulness in all situations is a major perspective adjuster when things might not be going the way we would like. When you choose to look at all the good things in life and all that life it has to offer, you begin to have a brighter outlook on your personal situation. I've heard it said that whatever we focus on we make bigger, and I find that to be true—and unfortunately it works equally for the bad as the good. I know it takes effort for me to stay on top of what I let roll around in my head, but I know one other thing for sure: the faster I stop focusing on a lost fish, the less likely the loss will change the course of my day.

Let's not focus or complain about the negatives or what we don't have but instead purpose to have a heart of gladness and gratitude for our many blessings. That is a benefit of applying 1 Thessalonians 5:18 to our lives.

James

HEBREWS 4:12

(NIV)

> For the word of God is alive and active. Sharper than any double-edged sword, It penetrates even to dividing soul and spirit, joints, and marrow; it judges the thoughts and attitudes of the heart.

There are a lot of elements that need to come together for a lure to actually catch a fish. The lure must be the correct color, shape, and size. It needs to have the correct wobble, buzz, and vibration, with all its parts in working order. However, the most important part of any lure is the hook. The hook is what ultimately get the job done. The hook connects to the fish so it can be hauled to the boat. One thing I've noticed about bass pros is that they always change the hooks on the lures—even on a new lure opened out of the package, the hook is immediately swapped for a new, sharper one. Pros know the importance of sharp hooks.

The book of Hebrews describes the Word of God as "sharper than any double-edged sword, it penetrates even to divide soul and spirit, joints, and marrow; it judges the thoughts and the attitudes of the heart." God uses the sharp penetrating power of His Word to bring us closer to him. The Bible is unlike any other book that has ever been written. No one reads a novel and says, "I think God is speaking to me," but countless thousands have read the Bible and concluded that God was speaking to them. Why? Because the Bible is the primary way God chooses to speak to our hearts.

The Word of God is sharp. Let it bring you closer to Him.

Do you struggle with reading God's Word? Make it a priority in your life starting today.

Chris

COLOSSIANS 3:23–24

(HCSB)

> Whatever you do, do it enthusiastically, as something done for the Lord and not for men, knowing that you will receive the reward of an inheritance from the Lord.

Over the years, I have been accused of getting a little too excited when I land a big fish in a tournament. I've heard things from fans like "Act like you've been there before" or "That's a little much." I've even landed a few descriptive words, like *chaos* or *freaking out*. I'll never forget a time when David Williams and I were battling it out for first place on Lewis Smith Lake in Alabama. He said, "I could hear you all the way down in the next cove every time you landed one." There's something that for me never gets dull about landing big fish, especially when money is on the line.

All in all, it goes back to the verse in Colossians that whatever you do, you should do it enthusiastically, as something done for the Lord and not men. It wouldn't matter if it was a ten-pounder, a three-pointer, a hole in one, or a home run in the bottom of the ninth, it will always feel the same to me. I constantly remind myself that I do what I do for men but to enthusiastically celebrate every single gift that's from above, including those green fish. I know every fish I catch is a gift, and I can't act like I'm not excited and thankful for every single one of them.

I don't celebrate to earn my inheritance from the Lord. I celebrate because of my inheritance from the Lord, and you can't hide the gratitude you receive from the grace that only God can give.

What are you going to do enthusiastically today?

Blake

HEBREWS 10:39

(NLT)

> But we are not like those who turn away from God to their own destruction. We are the faithful ones, whose souls will be saved.

I love to receive, hear, or read a good encouragement—something that builds me up or refreshes me along the way. Hebrews 10:39 does just that.

I enjoy a good movie. *Rudy* and *Braveheart* are among my all-time favorites. In *Braveheart*, I think of the scene where William Wallace is on horseback, his face painted blue and white, rallying the troops to stay the course when things don't look great and so many are tempted to walk away. He inspires them not to give up, and he challenges them that even if on that battlefield they give their lives, they will do it as free men. It is as the passage in Hebrews says: "But we are not like those who turn away from God to their own destruction. We are the faithful ones, whose souls will be saved."

I want to be one of the faithful ones through the changes and challenges of life. It is not going to be easy, but I know that God is worthy of it all.

Brothers in Christ, stand firm, persevere, and be the man of God He knows you can be and your family needs you to be. Blessings!

James

1 PETER 5:8

(ESV)

> Be sober-minded; be watchful. Your adversary the devil is prowling around like a roaring lion, seeking someone to devour.

Some time back, there was a debate in the fishing world as to who is the greatest fisherman of all time. Anyone who follows the pro fishing scene can probably guess the names that were in the running. Rick Clunn, Kevin Vandam, Roland Martin, Bill Dance, Jimmy Houston, Hank Parker, George Cochran, and Larry Nixon were among the list of the best anglers.

I have a pastor friend who has a very different idea on who the greatest fisherman of all time is. His answer is the Devil. He points out that Satan is the master at casting things in front of us that at first look good but after they're taken always lead us somewhere we didn't plan to go. Satan will also use us as lures to hook others in sin as well.

Most people today have a false image of the Devil. They often picture him as a red guy with a pitchfork who resides down in hell. The Bible tells us that Satan was perfect in beauty and has never been to hell. On the contrary, he lives on the earth and seeks to devour men.

My pastor friend brought to me a great challenge about the greatest fisherman who's ever lived. He said, "Don't allow Satan to use you, your spouse, or someone in your family to 'lure' someone into sin. You don't have to be following the Devil for him to use you."

Examine your walk with Christ today. Are there actions, thoughts, or even inaction that you are allowing Satan to use? If so, repent today and be filled with the Spirit of God.

Chris

LUKE 12:34

(HCSB)

> For where your treasure is, there your heart will be also.

I've never been one of those to have keepsakes or memorabilia from the past. As a kid, I moved around a lot after my parents divorced. I learned quickly that the more you kept, the more you had to carry. So after the sixth or seventh move, I remember getting rid of anything extra—all my little treasures, some might say. It taught me from a young age that everything around us is temporary and one day will be gone. Fortunately for me, I gave my life to Christ at a pretty young age, this one verse always stuck out to me: "Where your treasure is, your heart will be also." Where you build value is where you will place it, and God knows how much we as humans value things on earth. He knows we constantly try to build value for ourselves through the things we acquire.

How awesome it is that God took all the pressure off when He helped us understand that the best treasure we can acquire is our future home in heaven. A place were moth and rust cannot destroy. A place prepared by the King of Kings and Lord of Lords especially for me!

What treasures are you storing up for yourself? The temporary, or the Eternal?

Blake

JOHN 15:4

(NLT)

> Remain in me, and I will remain in you. For a branch cannot produce fruit if it is severed from the vine, and you cannot be fruitful unless you remain in me.

In my Bible, this scripture is in red lettering, which means that it is Jesus's own words. Jesus is telling us how important it is for us to stay connected to Him. There are so many ways that we can do that. We can find a local home church to attend regularly, along with Bible study groups, Sunday school, and the small groups some churches offer, which are great to build relationships and continually stay connected to God's Word (Bible apps are also helpful for this). On tour, we have the Fellowship of Christian Anglers, where a bunch of anglers meet up and hear a message from one of the anglers, and we submit prayer requests so that we can agree upon it corporately.

The Christian walk requires us to spend time with God, in His Word, and in prayer. It isn't like once we become Christians, we've arrived; but like anything else of value in life, it requires time. Purpose to make time for reading your Bible or praying.

Our relationship with Jesus is the most important thing, so we want it to be a vibrant one in which He continually speaks into our lives. This time is how we stay connected to the vine.

It has become clear to me that whenever I am not regularly spending time with God, my fuse is shorter with those around me. We all go through seasons in life when we are diligent and purposeful to make that time and stay connected, but there are times when life gets super busy, and we must put the brakes on things to reprioritize our time. Life truly has it highs and lows, its twists and turns, and if you're like me, you always hope that one day you'll arrive at your destination, having outrun the tough times. I've personally not found that to be the case.

What I find myself desiring is that when the next challenge comes around, I will handle it better as a follower of Jesus. The only way to do that is to remain in Him, and He will remain in you. It's important that no matter the challenge, I walk with Jesus.

James

GALATIANS 5:22–23

(NIV)

> But the fruit of the Spirit is love, joy, peace, forbearance, kindness, goodness, faithfulness, gentleness and self-control. Against such things there is no law.

There is an old question about fishermen that goes like this: "Do all fishermen lie? Or do all liars fish?" Fishermen aren't really known as the most honest people on the planet—least of all when it comes to where or how many and how big those fish actually were. Oftentimes that ten-pound bass actually weighed seven pounds!

I had a student of mine who had become a great fisherman refuse to tell me where he caught fish. He said, "I know you are a preacher, and I know when people ask you where you caught them you are not going to lie, so I can't tell you." And as hard as it is to get accurate information on whether fishermen actually *caught* fish or not, there is one telltale mark that can let you know the truth. If your buddy tells you he caught them, ask to look at his thumb. The mark of a bass fisherman will be revealed by the condition of his lipping thumb. A rough, torn-up thumb means he's telling the truth. A smooth thumb means you better look a little deeper into his story.

Just as bass fishermen will have the marks of truth on their thumbs, the true disciples of Christ should have the marks of discipleship in their lives. The Bible tells us there are marks that will show who the true disciples really are. One of those marks is the bearing of fruit. Every true disciple will produce the fruits of the Spirit of God. Galatians tells us those fruits are love, joy, peace, patience, kindness, goodness, faithfulness, gentleness, and self-control. The fruit of the Spirit of God should be evident to those who do not believe in the Christian life. It is one of the marks of the true believer.

Does what you say match how you live? Do you have the marks of a true disciple? Do a thumb check.

Chris